welcome baby

Sweet Dreams

Guest

Advice for Parents

Wishes for Baby

Sweet Dreams

Guest

Advice for Parents

- -

- -

- -

- -

Wishes for Baby

- -

- -

- -

- -

Sweet Dreams

Guest

Advice for Parents

Wishes for Baby

Sweet Dreams

Guest

Advice for Parents

Wishes for Baby

Sweet Dreams

Guest

Advice for Parents

Wishes for Baby

Sweet Dreams

Guest

Advice for Parents

Wishes for Baby

Sweet Dreams

Guest

Advice for parents

Wishes for Baby

Sweet Dreams

Guest

Advice for Parents

Wishes for Baby

Sweet Dreams

Guest

....

....

Advice for Parents

....

....

....

....

Wishes for Baby

....

....

....

....

Sweet Dreams

Guest

Advice for Parents

Wishes for Baby

Sweet Dreams

Guest

Advice for Parents

Wishes for Baby

Sweet Dreams

Guest

Advice for Parents

Wishes for Baby

Sweet Dreams

Guest

Advice for parents

Wishes for Baby

Sweet Dreams

Guest

Advice for Parents

Wishes for Baby

Sweet Dreams

Guest

Advice for parents

Wishes for Baby

Sweet Dreams

Guest

Advice for parents

Wishes for baby

Sweet Dreams

Guest

....

Advice for Parents

....

....

....

....

Wishes for Baby

....

....

....

....

Sweet Dreams

Guest

....

Advice for Parents

Wishes for Baby

Sweet Dreams

Guest

- -

Advice for Parents

- -

- -

- -

- -

Wishes for Baby

- -

- -

- -

Sweet Dreams

Guest

Advice for Parents

Wishes for Baby

Sweet Dreams

Guest

Advice for Parents

Wishes for Baby

Sweet Dreams

Guest

Advice for Parents

Wishes for Baby

Sweet Dreams

Guest

- -

Advice for Parents

- -

- -

- -

- -

Wishes for Baby

- -

- -

- -

Sweet Dreams

Guest

Advice for Parents

Wishes for Baby

Sweet Dreams

Guest

Advice for Parents

Wishes for Baby

Sweet Dreams

Guest

Advice for Parents

Wishes for Baby

Sweet Dreams

Guest

- -

Advice for Parents

- -

- -

- -

- -

Wishes for Baby

- -

- -

- -

Sweet Dreams

Guest

Advice for Parents

Wishes for Baby

Sweet Dreams

Guest

Advice for Parents

Wishes for Baby

Sweet Dreams

Guest

Advice for Parents

Wishes for Baby

Sweet Dreams

Guest

- -

- -

Advice for Parents

- -

- -

- -

Wishes for Baby

- -

- -

- -

Sweet Dreams

Guest

Advice for Parents

Wishes for Baby

Sweet Dreams

Guest

Advice for Parents

Wishes for Baby

Sweet Dreams

Guest

Advice for Parents

Wishes for Baby

Sweet Dreams

Guest

Advice for Parents

Wishes for Baby

Sweet Dreams

Guest

Advice for Parents

Wishes for Baby

Sweet Dreams

Guest

Advice for Parents

Wishes for Baby

Sweet Dreams

Guest

- -

Advice for Parents

- -

- -

- -

Wishes for Baby

- -

- -

- -

Sweet Dreams

Guest

- -

- -

Advice for Parents

- -

- -

- -

- -

Wishes for Baby

- -

- -

- -

- -

Sweet Dreams

Guest

_____

Advice for Parents

_____

_____

_____

Wishes for Baby

_____

_____

_____

Sweet Dreams

Guest

Advice for Parents

Wishes for Baby

Sweet Dreams

Guest

Advice for Parents

Wishes for Baby

Sweet Dreams

Guest

Advice for Parents

Wishes for Baby

Sweet Dreams

Guest

Advice for Parents

Wishes for Baby

Sweet Dreams

Guest

Advice for Parents

Wishes for Baby

Sweet Dreams

Guest

....

....

Advice for Parents

....

....

....

....

Wishes for Baby

....

....

....

Sweet Dreams

Guest

- -

- -

Advice for Parents

- -

- -

- -

- -

Wishes for Baby

- -

- -

- -

Sweet Dreams

Guest

Advice for Parents

Wishes for Baby

Sweet Dreams

Guest

Advice for Parents

Wishes for Baby

Sweet Dreams

Guest

Advice for parents

Wishes for Baby

Sweet Dreams

Guest

Advice for Parents

- -

- -

- -

- -

Wishes for Baby

- -

- -

- -

- -

Sweet Dreams

Guest

Advice for Parents

- -

- -

- -

- -

Wishes for Baby

- -

- -

- -

- -

Sweet Dreams

Guest

Advice for Parents

Wishes for Baby

Sweet Dreams

Guest

Advice for Parents

Wishes for Baby

Sweet Dreams

Guest

Advice for Parents

Wishes for Baby

Sweet Dreams

Guest

Advice for parents

Wishes for baby

Sweet Dreams

Guest

Advice for parents

Wishes for Baby

Sweet Dreams

Guest

Advice for Parents

Wishes for Baby

Sweet Dreams

Guest

Advice for Parents

Wishes for Baby

Sweet Dreams

Guest

Advice for Parents

- -

- -

- -

- -

Wishes for Baby

- -

- -

- -

Sweet Dreams

Guest

Advice for Parents

Wishes for Baby

Sweet Dreams

Guest

Advice for Parents

Wishes for Baby

Sweet Dreams

Guest

Advice for Parents

Wishes for Baby

Sweet Dreams

Guest

Advice for Parents

Wishes for Baby

Sweet Dreams

Guest

....

....

Advice for parents

....

....

....

....

Wishes for baby

....

....

....

....

Sweet Dreams

Guest

Advice for Parents

Wishes for Baby

Sweet Dreams

Guest

Advice for Parents

- -

- -

- -

- -

Wishes for Baby

- -

- -

- -

Sweet Dreams

Guest

Advice for Parents

Wishes for Baby

Sweet Dreams

Guest

- -

Advice for Parents

- -

- -

- -

- -

Wishes for Baby

- -

- -

- -

- -

Sweet Dreams

Guest

Advice for Parents

Wishes for Baby

Sweet Dreams

Guest

Advice for Parents

Wishes for Baby

Sweet Dreams

Guest

Advice for Parents

- -

- -

- -

Wishes for Baby

- -

- -

- -

Sweet Dreams

Guest

....

....

Advice for Parents

....

....

....

....

Wishes for Baby

....

....

....

Sweet Dreams

Guest

....

Advice for Parents

....

....

....

....

Wishes for Baby

....

....

....

Sweet Dreams

Guest

- -

- -

Advice for Parents

- -

- -

- -

- -

Wishes for Baby

- -

- -

- -

- -

Sweet Dreams

Guest

Advice for Parents

Wishes for Baby

Sweet Dreams

Guest

Advice for Parents

- -

- -

- -

- -

Wishes for Baby

- -

- -

- -

- -

Sweet Dreams

Guest

....

....

Advice for Parents

Wishes for Baby

Sweet Dreams

Guest

....

....

Advice for Parents

....

....

....

....

Wishes for Baby

....

....

....

....

Sweet Dreams

Guest

Advice for Parents

Wishes for Baby

Gift Log Tracker

Gift from...	Gift Description

Gift Log Tracker

Gift from...	Gift Description

Gift Log Tracker

Gift from...   **Gift Description**

Gift Log Tracker

Gift from...	Gift Description

Gift Log Tracker

Gift from...	Gift Description

Gift Log Tracker

Gift from...	Gift Description

Just one more
Chapter
Thank you!

We hope you enjoyed our book.

As a small family company, your feedback is very important to us .

Please let us know how you like our book at :

pickme.readme@gmail.com